ARISE
TO
PRAYING
GOD'S
WORD

ARISE TO PRAYING GOD'S WORD

BARBARA HOLMES

ISBN:	Hardcover	978-1-9845-3727-0
	Softcover	978-1-9845-3726-3
	eBook	978-1-9845-3725-6

Print information available on the last page.

Rev. date: 06/30/2018

To order additional copies of this book, contact:
Xlibris
1-888-795-4274
www.Xlibris.com
Orders@Xlibris.com
759885

Did you know that there are some prayer warriors who do not know how to pray? This is what the devil likes, he wants to close the mouths of the people of prayer. To be an effective prayer warrior, scriptures need to be used in prayer. One of the reasons the world is in the condition it's in is not putting confidence and trust in the scriptures. Did you know it takes Christian intercessors to open the door to the will of God? Christians who have been born again and filled with the Holy Spirit have been given all the authority they need to access heaven. Effective prayer will only happen when intercessors learn to arise in prayer. One of the most important things that people of prayer need to learn is how to pray according to the Word of God. For too long, people of prayer have not prayed God's Word in their prayers and supplication. Prayer should not be based on feelings and thoughts but on the Word of God. Effective prayers must be done according to the principles of faith in the Word of God.

In the scripture Hebrews 11:1 (King James Version), it states, "Now faith is the substance of things hoped for, the evidence of thing not seen." In the scriptures, when praying, faith must be used, like the title deed document, which is your given authorization. In the scriptures, when praying, faith is your main ingredient, your legal document. God is saying to us to use his Word in our prayer request. The more Word we have, the more faith will develop in that Word and in him.

According to the *Strong's Exhaustive Concordance of the Bible* (the Greek dictionary)—index to the New Testament—the Greek word *elpizo* means "hope for, to hope, put hope in, expect, an attitude of confidently looking forward to what is good and beneficial." What good things have you been looking for? Are you looking for family members to get saved or healed from cancer or something else? Then foresee this thing happening. It means expectation and anticipation, with the full assurance of the Word backing you up. Faith will bring into reality those things that are unrealistic. You may be hoping that every bill is paid in full. Your faith will give you an assurance that every need is met and every bill is paid. Your hope will transform from hope to faith when your confidence and trust is in God's Word. As believers, we believe what his Word says because the reliance is in him. In the scriptures, when praying, faith must be used, like the title deed document and authorization. Faith in God's Word must be used right now. The purpose of this book is to tell all people of prayer that we must arise to praying God's Word and use our authority and not allow the devil to defeat us.

Prayer is more than just communicating with God; it must be done according to the principles of faith, in the Word of God, in order to be effective. In the scripture Hebrews 11:1 KJV, it states, "Now faith is the substance of things hoped for, the evidence of things not seen." In prayer, faith must be in the title deed. In the scriptures, faith is your main ingredient, which is needed in prayer. Faith is your legal document, your document of authorization. God is saying to us to use his Word. God's will is his word. The more prayer warriors have God's Word in them, the more their faith will develop in that Word. Faith does not come from the five senses—what you see, what you hear, what you smell, what you taste, and what you touch. It is based on the Word of God.

The Greek word for *faith*, according to the *Strong's Exhaustive Concordance*, is *hypostasis* (*hyo* meaning "under" and *histeni* meaning "to stand"). It means that faith is the hypostasis. It is what we stand upon, the foundation that gives support. Faith in the scriptures will give the support that is needed when things are not looking good in your home, in your body, in your marriage, in your church, or even in your finances. Faith in the Word means having confidence and trust in the scriptures. It is what you stand upon and what you believe when you don't see anything happening in the natural world. You know that there is something happening in the spirit realm because you believe God's Word. Your confidence is in what he has said.

Faith says, "I receive it now in Jesus's name." This is when things will begin to change here on earth and a shift will begin to take place. Prayer is not one of those "maybe God will hear me one day." No! Or a hit-and-miss. As people of prayer, we should be getting answers. People of prayer are needed now more than ever before. In 2 Corinthians 4:4 KJV, it states, "In whom the god of this world [which is Satan] has blinded the minds of them which believe not, lest the light of the Glorious Gospel of Christ, Who is the image of God, should shine on them." As believers, we must understand that the only way the will of God can be done on planet earth is when we, as people of prayer, give him consent and give him authorization right now.

There are some who think God is in control and he got. Well, that is wrong! Wrong! Wrong! Why do you think the world is in such a mess—abortions, murders of young children, stabbings and murders of young girls? Racism is on the rise. There are more crimes, and more people are facing economic problems. If we, as the body of intercessors, give the Lord Jesus Christ the consent he needs, we will see miracles for prosperity and wealth, people being delivered from drugs and alcohol, and our youth being delivered from gang activity. We will come behind in nothing. The world will come to us and know that we have been with Jesus.

According to Acts 4:13 KJV, "Now when they saw the boldness of Peter and John, and perceived that they were unlearned and ignorant men, they marveled; and they took note concerning them that they had been with Jesus." The people at that time knew that these men had not been rabbinical to higher learning, but they saw their boldness. *Boldness* is from the Greek word, according to *The Outline Bible Five Translation* and *Practical Word Studies in the New Testament Volume 1* (A–K, 416), *parresian*, which means "to enter God's presence freely and openly with confidence and assurance" (p. 222).

As people of prayer, there is an assurance of what the people of God should have and what the world needs to marvel at. The boldness that Peter and John had was because they knew that God loved that man who was born lame from his mother's womb, and they acted upon the Holy Ghost. It was time for him to arise in the name of Jesus. Most importantly, Jesus was in them. And because he was in them, what they believed him for, he would perform.

The next chapter (v. 14) states, "But seeing the man who was healed standing with them, they had nothing to say." This man whom Peter and John saw was crippled and needed healing, and he received it. Peter boldly spoke the Word and said, "Rise up and walk." Peter took him by the right hand and raised him up. Immediately, the crippled man's feet and ankles were strengthened. Jumping up, he stood and walked and entered the temple with them. Praise God!

People need to know and see the anointing and power of prayer working in the lives of men and women. People of prayer, the world needs to see our faith at work. Peter's and John's faith was at work. They had no doubt in their heart when they saw the lame man at the temple gate. The reason their faith was at work was because they put God's

Word first. His Word should be the absolute, final authority. People of prayer, God's Word is the cure and antidote for what is wrong. This is why we must pray the Word.

In Proverbs 4:20–22 KJV, it states, " ²⁰ My son, attend to my words; incline your ear to my sayings. ²¹ Do not let them depart from your eyes; keep them in the midst of your heart; ²² for they are life to those who find them, and health to all their body." What is this scripture talking about, and why is it important to men and women of prayer?

A. "My son, attend to my words . . ." What does that mean? It means that as believers, the Word of God is our authority, and it needs to be put first. When people are going through certain situations and circumstances, they will need praying people who have put the Word of God first in their situation, condition, and circumstance. The Hebrew word for *attend*, in the Hebrew Bible lexicon 10.H7181, is *qashab* (*kawshab*, a primitive root) meaning "to hear, be attentive, heed, incline of ears, attend of ears, hearken, pay attention, listen." *Qal* means "incline, attend of ears, hearken, pay attention, listen." *Hiphil* means "to pay attention, give attention," a primitive root to prick up the ears that hearken or attend.

If we are to be effective prayer warriors, we must attend our ears to his Word each and every day. Pay attention. When we arise in the morning, we need to spend time with the Lord before we leave and start our day. His Word must prick our ears. I know it is very tempting to turn on the news and different morning shows and even the soaps. But when we arise, we need God's Word on our mind. In life, we don't know who will need us and who will want us to pray for them and who may be on the verge of suicide or who may want to just destroy their life and other people's lives. If we are going to do the will of God, he needs our complete attention. So many times our attention is divided. But our Lord wants our undivided attention.

B. He goes on to say, "Incline thine ear unto my says . . ." What he is saying is that our ears need to be open. This is not just our natural ears but our spiritual ears. So many times our ears are clogged with what we have heard. Some of us have heard fear, doubt, and God put sickness on us. No, the devil wants people to have a distorted view of God. When it comes to praying God's Word, we need to unlearn some things, which we were taught in the past, down from ages and centuries, even some religious teachings. Listen to this, prayer warriors, when it comes to the promises of God, the devil wants to take it from you as well as the person you are praying for. The Word of God belongs to all people. The promises of God are sure. The Lord wants our ears opened to him. Because when we are open to what he is saying, he can work through us. But we must be accessible to what he is saying.

C. "Let them not depart from thine eyes [God's Word]. He goes into thine eyes. See it every day and every night and every waking moment." We are to keep his Word before our eyes. It means that whatever situation someone finds themselves in, we, as people of prayer, must go to the scripture. Pray the scriptures and confess the scriptures. For example, if you're praying for someone who is sick, take them to the Word of God. I am not saying to be insensitive to what they are saying or what they say the doctor has told them. But they must know the Lord loves them enough to have done something about their condition over thousand years ago.

Isaiah 53:5 KJV states, "But He was wounded for our transgressions, He was bruised our iniquities: the chastisement of our peace was upon Him; and with His strips we our healed." Let them see in the scripture that they were healed on that cross (past tense) thousand years ago. Show them they must keep the scriptures before them and must keep confessing it out of their mouth. Let them know he loved them so much until every sickness and disease was on the cross with Jesus. And he took it to the cross on his body so they would not have to. Praise God!

As they keep that Word before them and confess it out of their mouth, they will begin to see themselves healed! People need to know that God loves them enough to heal them and set them free from any kind of burden. Have them confess Isiah 53:5, "And with his stripes I am heal in Jesus name." And also, have them confess "Jesus took my infamies and bore all of my diseases" (Matthew 8:17). Have them confess that it is not the will of God for them to be sick with cancer, diabetes, high blood pressure, kidney failure, back problems, or lung problems! In the name of Jesus, I curse every sickness and disease that has come upon this body. I command it to leave right now!

Satan, I serve you notice right now that this body is not his prosperity. This body belongs to God. And confess Isaiah 54:7, "No weapon that is form against you shall prosper!" No weapon of cancer shall prosper! No weapon of kidney failure shall prosper! No weapon of anxiety or fear shall proper! No weapon of lung disease shall proper! No heart disease or ringing in the ear shall proper! Every weapon that has come up against this body is destroyed and every assignment of the devil is demolished in Jesus's name, I speak healing over this body. I don't care if you suffer from aortic aneurysms, dissections, ruptures, back pains, or swollen joints. Command the devil to take his hands off that part of your body.

People of prayer, our assignment is to let the people know that the Word of God is a building block of faith. And when more people are built up in the Word of God, which is faith in the Word, this blocks the devil from getting in. Praise God. So whatever the sickness or disorder or complaints—such as strokes, tumors, germ cell tumors, benign tumor, lymphoma, and leukemia, whatsoever—the problem is that it's coming against the health. Intercessory prayer warriors, we must let them know and the sickness know that they may take their medication, but there is another medication—which is the Word of God.

The scripture states in Job 22:28 KJV, "Thou shalt also decree a thing, and it shall be established unto thee: and the light shall shine upon thy ways." When there is someone who will continually affirm what God's Word says out of their mouth, the supernatural power of God will be established in that body, and the power of God's Word will start working in that body to eradicate that sickness. Confess 1 Peter 2:24 KJV, "Who His own Self bear our sins in His Own Body on the tree, that we, being dead to sins, should live unto Righteousness: by whose strips you were healed." Jesus paid the penalty in full price for our spirits to be healed, as well as for the body and emotions to be healed.

Before Kenneth Hagin learned about faith, I can remember reading a story about him in *God's Medicine* (1977). According to Hagin (1977), he said he could see himself in the casket (p. 15). Some individuals see themselves dead. There are some whom the doctors have given up on, and they, too, have given up on life. They need to hear a healing word from a man or woman of God. They need to hear from God's intercessors, God is interested in people being well in their bodies. Why must we be ready? Because there are times when life beats people down so hard that they are at the crossroads of life. They don't know which way to go, and if they make the wrong decision, it can affect the whole course of their life. We will meet people whose lives have hit a crisis and who are facing trauma. The grace of God will give us what to say.

The scriptures states in 1 Peter 3:15 KJV, "Be ready always to give an answer to every man that asketh you a reason of the hope that is in you with meekness and fear." Some people have lost hope and faith, but God has predestined for people to win. But the enemy wants them to lose. God has blessed human beings with the ability to make a choice. Some make the wrong choices, but because of Jesus, they can make the right choice. We must let them know these things. But God has a will that people will win, and he will bring forth his purpose in their lives. People need to bring forth their purpose. The devil does not want them to fulfil the plan that God has before them. People will come to us for answers, and we can lead them to Christ through the scriptures and give them the counsel they need. Whatever the Word says, we cannot allow it to depart from our eyes. As people of God, we must know that the Holy Ghost leads and directs us to his Word.

Now let's go back to Proverbs 4:21, "And let it not depart out from your eyes." When it comes to being a prayer warrior, we must push out stuff that is not in line with the Word of God. There are so many things that try to take God's place. Get your perception correct. Your harvest is white and ready.

This is the time for blessings; this is the time to be a blessing to as many humans as possible. Some people we will meet are in a dilemma, and we have what it takes for them to come out of their problems. The devil is afraid for you to open your mouth and use the Word. Prayer warriors, we must tell people that they don't have to fail!

D. "Keep them [God's Words] in the midst of thine heart." What that means is, the word must be in our spirits so we can get God's kind of results. Praise the Lord Jesus Christ! As people of prayer, the Word of God will bring forth those godly results.

E. "For they are life unto those that find them, and health to all their flesh." God's Word is filled with energy and powerful substance. The Word of God will cause you to change your image, and you will give birth to the Word of God, which you have been placing before your eyes and out of your mouth. As you keep that Word before you, the Holy Ghost will impart his life-giving strength into you. But the main principle is to stay focused on the Word. Listen, people of prayer, when it comes to where we get our authority and power from, it is from the Holy Ghost and from the authority of the Word of God. When these two are combined, this will connect us to the revelation knowledge of Jesus Christ. All Jesus Christ does is in the Word of God. Through the power of the Holy Ghost, we receive everything. He is in us. God has predestinated every prayer warrior to know in his Word and take authority by using the Word.

According to Ephesians 6:12 KJV, "For we wrestle not against flesh and blood, but against principalities, against powers, against rulers of the darkness of this world, against spiritual wickedness in high places."

The devil uses evil spirits to control human beings. But thank God, prayer warriors, for he has given us authority over them even in the lives of others so they can come to Christ, in Jesus's name. Paul wrote this so that we would understand this, being Christians. Our fight is not against people, and as people of prayer, individuals need to know the individuals. Society at large is not the enemy, but the devil is the adversary, the enemy of all humans.

God at this time wants his people of prayer to arise and be on fire and be full of the power of the Holy Ghost to burst through the lives of men and women and to heal, deliver, and set people free. There are people who want to be free from welfare and other types of assistance. The devil's assignment is to keep them poor and needy and discouraged, which leads to poverty and mental illness. There are so many people who are tired and worn out from living paycheck to paycheck. In the name of Jesus, we must decree and declare that every assignment of the enemy to keep your finances tied up is destroyed!

The Bible states in Joel 2:25 KJV, "And I will restore to you the years that the locust hath eaten, the cankerworm, and the caterpillar, and the palmerworm, my great army which I sent among you." God is a restorer. In 2018, according to the *Strong's Hebrew Lexicon* 7999, *shalam* (*shaw-lam*, a primitive root) means "to be safe." In God, you are safe and you will be unharmed. Meaning he will compensate you for your loss, and he will give to you again. Also, he will give you something in your body, in your mind, or in the palms of your hand, which you never had before. God designed for his people to be blessed. God wants to restore something that you lost, and he is going to use the prayer warriors as his instruments. There are individuals who have been on welfare and have lived in poverty, and some have no insurance because they cannot afford it. God is interested in the totality of the person. There is no part of their life that God is not interested in.

The book of Joel talks about "the years the locust has eaten." According to Swaggart's *Expositor's Study Bible* (2007–2010), "'And I will restore to you the years' refers to that period of time which began with Nebuchadnezzar and which now has lasted for about 2,500 years. The mention of the locust etc., is meant to be symbolic of years lost to the 'times of Gentiles.' The phrase 'My great army which I sent among you,' speaks of the empire which ruled Israel because of Israel's sin and refusal to repent" (p. 1,532). God is so good he will restore the years they have lost because of their own ignorance, or their not knowing what they were doing. There are some people who feel that they have wasted their time and energy, and they feel like they are failures, that their life is totally lost. The devil tells them that they are no good, and they allow their conscience to beat them up. Some of them have lost their finances, even their place to stay, and some are living in shelters, even in streets. But as an intercessor, we are to stand in the gap for them so whatever they lost, God will restore it to them.

As an intercessor, we are to stand in the gap between that person, or it may be persons. They may have done wrong, or there may have been some wrongdoings and misbehaviors. They may have been disobedient also. But because of the urging of the Holy Ghost that prompts the intercessor to intercede for them, God begins to work on them and deliver their minds and emotions and their finances. You see, the devil wants people to give up and doubt God, but God can intervene in their lives. The defined intercessor is to stand in the gap in prayer, standing on scripture or scriptures on behalf of other people who may have triggered judgment on themselves because of their sinful acts.

Let's decree right now in the name of Jesus. Father, forgive us and others who have given their time over to the devil, in Jesus's name. Father, we decree right now, in Jesus's name, we, as well as others, will repent before you. In the name of Jesus, the spirit of poverty is destroyed off their lives, and the spirit of poverty and insecurity is destroyed! In the name of Jesus, decree and declare Galatians 3:13 KJV, "Christ has redeemed me from the curse of the Law." When Christ was on the cross, he was paying the penalty for mankind's financial freedom also. People of prayer, say this out of your mouth, decree it over your life, and decree it over the lives of people you know who are struggling in their finances. Confess out of your mouth, and have them confess out of their mouth.

According to Galatians 3:13 KJV, Christ has redeemed me from the curse of the devil's assignment on the finances, and in the name of Jesus, I will destroy the curse of being poverty-stricken, the curse of not having enough, and the curse of being needy. We decree and declare that whatever held us back in 2000, 2010, 2011, 2012, etc., what held you back even before 2000 and even during the time of your birth, will not hold you back in 2018. The enemy

In the scripture Joel 2:25 KJV, according to *The Kenneth Copeland Word of Faith Study Bible*, it states, "And I will compensate you for the years the locusts have eaten and the fledging locust my great army which I sent against you." The introduction of this scripture introduces a prophet by the name of Joel. Prophet Joel warned Judah of the plague of locusts that would eat up all their livestock, cattle, bulls, oxen, cows, sheep, and horses. And also, the enemy would come in and destroy their vineyards. Their vegetables were extinguished, along with their fields with wheat and barley. The locust was described as a limitless human army. This was the judgment brought against them due to their disobedience. But Joel let them know that if they would repent to God and change their way of thinking about God and obey his Word through his prophets, he would restore to them all they had lost. This meant that the great outpouring of the Holy Spirit would rain upon the land.

Prayer warriors, our obedience to giving our monies is tied to our financial wealth. Just like others, giving is connected to coming out of poverty. As people who pray God's Word, we must be in position to tell them. In this story, Judah's disobedience to God caused them to go into financial ruin. When people do not want to pay their tithes and offering to support the kingdom of God or when people do not want to support their pastors financially or support other ministries with their finances, they open the door for financial devastation. The government does not want to support people, and if the president wants to cut all the aid to people, he can. We, as people of prayer, must intercede for them so that they will repent in Jesus's name. And if we have to be guilty of it, we will repent ourselves.

Father, in Jesus's name, we pray Ephesians 1:17 KJV, "That the God of our Lord Jesus Christ, the Father of Glory, may give unto you the Spirit of Wisdom and Revelation in the knowledge of Him." Prayer warriors, we receive knowledge of Christ from the Word of God that will catapult to increase in wisdom from that Word. Wisdom from that Word will give us the increased revelation knowledge. Let's go back a little bit to Ephesians 1:16 KJV, "Cease not to give thanks for you, making mention of you in my prayers." Paul was not just praying for the church of Ephesians, he was praying for the whole body of Christ and that we would walk in our authority and power.

Prayer warriors, because we have been born again, we received all the spiritual blessings because we have received Jesus and his name that gave us power over every unclean demon in the airwaves. The enemy works hard against people of prayer. He does not want them to know who is inside of them. Prayer warriors, he wants to keep us from knowing the truth, but tell the devil that he is a liar! God has given you, men and women of prayer, the supremacy and authority that is needed in this world to fight against the devil and his demons so we can control him. His glory days are over with. It's time we take what rightfully belongs to us. Paul had this great revelation—that we, as believers, have been given authority. It says in the book of Ephesians 1:1 that Paul, an apostle of Jesus Christ, was called out to be a special messenger. He was called out by God to dispatch his Word.

People of God, we have been dispatched by God through his grace to be his special messengers. The scripture goes on to say "by the will of God." Listen and hear, intercessors. It is by the will and authority and power of God that we are called to intercede for this country, intercede for President Trump, intercede for our young black men who are being killed, and intercede because racial tense is at an all-time high. Just like God called Paul, he is calling us. It also says in Ephesians 1:1–3 KJV, "To all the Saints which are at Ephesus, and the Faithful in Christ Jesus, Grace be to you, and peace from God our Father and from our Lord. Blessed be the God of our Lord Jesus Christ and Father of Glory Who has blessed us with all spiritual blessings in Heavenly places." This means every blessing there is belongs to the body of Christ. He said it in his Word. It is very important, people of prayer, that we get this. That means healing, deliverance, and finances. It is sad when we, as the body of Christ, will not arise and take what belongs to us. This is why there are people in the body of Christ who die early, die in poverty, or are angry at the church. Some die angry at God with unforgivenness.

This passage is talking about every spiritual thing there is. Jesus placed it in our hands. He placed healing in our hands, ideas to get wealth in our hands, and deliverance. As believers, we need to know and act on what belongs to us. As warriors of prayer, we must know the truth of the Word of God. John 8:32 KJV states, "And ye shall know the truth, and the truth shall make you free." The truth of the Word of God leads us out of bondage and tradition.

Now let's get back to Ephesians 1:4 KJV, "According as He has chosen us in him, before the foundation of the world." This means before our mothers and fathers got together, we were on his mind to fulfill the plan of salvation because of what Jesus did on the cross. Paul went on to say that in verse 5, we were predestinated. In *Strong's Concordance,* **προορίσας** ἡμᾶς εἰ in the Greek New Testament means God has determined beforehand that we, the body of Christ and people of prayer, would speak the things of God and walk in his authority, walk in God's ordained destiny and be able to help others through prayer and intercession, and walk in God's ordained purpose and fulfill the plans God has for them. It is such a disgrace to God, when we disobey his word. Jesus Christ bleed and died that people would live a healthy long life, but instead people are dying early in life because the people of prayer will not rise up against the authority of the devil who wants to destroy the lives of men and women, boys and girls. Ephesians 1:4 KJV states, "According as he has chosen us." We have been chosen and empowered and impacted to carry out his plans. It also says in Ephesians 1:9 KJV, "Having made known unto us the mystery of his will." When you pray the Word of God, you open the door to revelation knowledge and you set spiritual laws in motion. And the things that you speak according to the Word of God, you will witness it come to pass in Jesus name.

Ephesians 1:15–23 KJV states, " ¹⁵ Therefore also, after hearing of your faith in the Lord Jesus and your love toward all the saints, ¹⁶ do no cease giving thanks for you, mentioning you in my prayers." This is what Paul was praying for the church in Ephesians, but just like he prayed it for the church in Ephesus, he also prayed it for us. And now it is time that we, as people of prayer, begin to pray this prayer, speaking it and believing it! Paul had a revelation that the body of Christ still do not have. Here it is in verse 17: "So that the God of our Lord Jesus Christ,

Father of glory, may give you the Spirit of wisdom and revelation in the knowledge of him." What Paul was praying about here was that the saints of God, as people of God, would be able to judge and know who is living inside of us, which is Christ Jesus. And when we, as people of prayer, arise in prayer, we would know it is him that is backing us when we step out in authority on his Word and use it in prayer. The spirit of wisdom, which is based on the Word of God, is what Paul wanted us to know based on knowledge, which is information that comes from the message from what Jesus did on the cross. From his Word, we will be able to judge and discern with biblical insight from the Holy Ghost and revelation from God. It is high time we receive increased revelation to the fullest.

Verse 18 states, "The eyes of our understanding being enlighten." The eyes are talking about our heart and our spirit. When we start studying the Word and speaking the Word of God on a constant, consistent, prayerful basis rooted in the Word of God, things will begin to change. Our heart and our spirit will receive what it needs. Also, we will begin to walk in revelation knowledge of the Word of God. As we believe it, we will walk in the blessing, and the Word will cause us to walk in the anointed power of God. We, as people of prayer, will realize that God has given us authority through his Word to put the devil under our feet and to release people who have been in bondage for years.

Listen, when we have faith in the Word and believe it and speak it, we become movers in the atmosphere. We begin to suture things up. And as movers with faith in God's Word, there is nothing the enemy can do about it because the revelation knowledge we receive from the Word opens the door for the Holy Spirit. This is why it says in verse 18 that "the eyes of your understanding being enlighten." In *Strong's Exhaustive Concordance*, the Greek word *photizo* means "to give light, shine, give light, illuminate." It also means "to come to light and make clear." Let's shed some light on the word. As born-again believers, we are enemies of the devil. And as we carry the Word of God and pray and speak it, individuals' lives are changed.

Satan wants you to go by what you see, but because of your faith in the Word and because you speak it out loud, things begin to change. God will back you up because you are walking and operating in the power of the Holy Ghost. As prayer warriors, there are too many believers who do not believe that the Spirit of God, which is the authority of God, gives them the power to do what God has commanded them to do.

As people of prayer, the body of Christ is missing out on the supernatural working power of God. People of God, it is time that the glory of God be revealed through us. As the body of Christ, God wants us to be enlightened on who we are. In other words, he wants the light of who lives inside of us. God does not get the glory when his children are spiritually blind and miss out on what belongs to them. This is why in the continuation of Ephesians 1:18–23 KJV, it says, " [18] That you may know what is the hope of his calling, and what is the riches of the glory of His inheritance in the Saints, [19] And what is the exceeding greatness of his power to us-ward who believe, according to the working of His mighty power, [20] Which He wrought in Christ, when He raised Him from the dead and set Him at His Own Right Hand in the Heavenly places, [21] Far above all principality, and power and might, and dominion, and every name that is named, not only in this world, but also in that which is to come. [22] And has put all things under his feet, and gave Him to be the Head over all things to the Church, [23] Which is His Body, the fullness of Him that fills all in all."

If the power of God did not raise Jesus from the dead, the whole world would be in hell right now. The most important thing that happened to the whole world and especially the body of Christ was when Jesus was raised from the dead. This was a slap to the devil's face. The devil thought he had Jesus, and he thought he could keep the authority that Adam gave to him. But the devil is a liar. When Jesus was raised from the dead, he took Satan's authority, and he did it openly. And this is what we, as people or prayer, must get. Jesus took Satan's authority and gave it to us. When Jesus died on the cross and he rose from the dead, everything we, the people of prayer, needed was paid for. So we speak and think the Word, and things will manifest from it because his Spirit lives inside of us. In verse 22, let's reiterate when Jesus "put all things under his feet," which means all things were under the feet of the body of Christ. Sickness is under our feet, cancer is under our feet, high blood pressure is under our feet, liver and kidney diseases are under our feet, and the murder of our young black men is under our feet.

Jesus has given the church the authority we need. As people of prayer, we can oppose Satan and his demons. The power of the Holy Spirit will cause us to walk in the supernatural. Colossians 2:13–15 KJV states, " 13 And you, being dead in your sins, and the uncircumcision of the flesh, has He quicken together with Him." Before we got saved, we died in our sins. We did anything and everything we wanted to do because our spirit man was in the dark and we were no longer in the image of God. We were in the image of Satan. We had a sinful nature that was darkened. We were separated from God at that time, but when we became born again, we became spiritually alive. Now, people of prayer, because we are spiritually alive. Listen, what Jesus did on the cross caused us to be spiritually alive because Jesus's blood on the cross made it possible for sin to be forgiven. Thank you, Jesus. Our sins have been forgiven over a thousand years ago.

In Colossians 2:14 KJV, it states, "Blotting out the handwriting of the Ordinance that was against us, which was contrary to us, and took it out of the way nailing it to the cross." This means that the law of Moses was against us. God's rule and standard of holiness and righteousness was against mankind. It could not be reached by efforts alone. But when Jesus came, died, and was raised from the dead, he abolished it. He removed it from us. We could not keep the law. Jesus had to do it for us by being nailed to the cross. The law was done away with through the death of Christ.

Now let's go to Colossians 2:15 KJV: "And having spoiled principalities and powers He made a show of them openly, triumphing over them." Christ spoiled the plot of the devil and his demons on the cross and took his authority from him. Jesus embarrassed the devil openly on earth and also in heaven. Jesus defeated the enemy when he was raised from the dead. Paul got this revelation, and he wanted people of prayer to get this revelation also.

In the times that we are living in, people of prayer, this authority—through speaking the Word in prayer and believing it and confessing it—can no longer be ignored. I don't care how educated you are or how smart you are. When we arise to walk in prayer from authority from the Word of God, this must be spiritually discerned by faith in the Word of God. In Ephesians 2:1 KJV, it states, "And you has He quicken who were dead in trespasses and sin." In verse 1, it talks about how Jesus made us alive though the power of the Holy Ghost. This is what Paul is telling us. We have been made alive when Jesus was raised from the dead. He raised us up also. With him now, we are seated together in heavenly places.

Verse 2 states, "Wherein time past you walked according to the course of this world." In time past, we walked according to our flesh, our five senses, our lower nature, our sensations and perceptions (or what stimulates us). When we are one with Christ, intercessors, we are seated together with him. We are copartners with him. Jesus Christ is the head, and we, the people of prayer, are the body of Christ. The anointing that has come from the head has run down to the body. What is on the head is on the body. As people of prayer, we must believe that his authority is within us! Repeat this: "In the name of Jesus, we are one with Christ, and we have been raised up together with Christ!"

People of prayer, we must speak and know what belongs to Jesus Christ. It also belongs to us. Also, we, as people of prayer, have the faith and authority from the Holy Ghost. People of prayer, we must live by this realization in order for our prayers to be effective. The scripture asserts in 1 Corinthians 6:17 KJV, "But he that is join unto the Lord is one spirit." We are spiritually one with Christ, so we can do what God has called us to do. He has equipped us to do his work. Therefore, the Spirit tells us in 1 Corinthians 6:20 KJV, "For you are bought with a price; therefore Glorify God in your body." This scripture means that as people of prayer, we are not just any old body. Our status has changed. He has washed us and cleansed us with his Word, and we belong to the Lord. He paid the price for our freedom with his blood at Calvary. You need to confess and speak this right now: "I belong to God because Jesus paid the price for my freedom on Calvary. Therefore, I decree and declare I am free, in Jesus's name."

Therefore, begin to glorify God with your whole heart and speak it out of your mouth. People of prayer, remember what the Word of God communicates to us and that it encourages us to know this. In the book of Jeremiah 29:11 KJV, it states, "For I know the thoughts that I think toward you, says the Lord, thoughts of peace and not evil to bring us to an expected end." God, before the foundation of the world, has designed a blueprint for our lives. As prayer warriors, we must realize this, and we need to open up our eyes and know God has a plan for our lives. In order to get the plan, we must go by his Word. God never designed men and women to walk around poor, disgusting, or full of fear and worry. That is not God.

The Bible assures us in Ephesians 2:6 KJV, "And he has raised us up together, and made us sit together in Heavenly Places." When Jesus was raised from the dead, meaning he ascended from the grave into heaven, what he did was he transmitted his authority to us people of prayer, to the body of Christ! You need to give God praise for Christ transferred to the body of Christ, to us, his power and authority. Christ, at this time, is seated at the right hand of God; therefore, he has given to us what he walked and talked in.

Let's go over to Luke 10:19 KJV: "Behold, I give you Authority." The word *behold* in *Strong's Exhaustive Concordance of the Bible* (the Greek dictionary)—index 2400 to the New Testament—is *idou*, which means "to look." Jesus was saying to his disciples and telling us, people of prayer, that God has given us authority. Demons must submit to the authority and power that God has given to us. We need to thank God for what he has given to us. This is the victory he has given to us.

In Luke 9:1 KJV, it states, "Then He called His Twelve Disciples together, and gave them power and authority over all devils and to cure disease." God has given us, as people of prayer, a divine assignment over spirits of gloom and darkness that cause fear and worry. God has given us authority over depression, generational curses, and spirits of suicide. God has given us his power over them, and he has given us the authority that they can infiltrate our families and our churches or our cities. In Jesus's name, we take this authority and anointing over our country and states. The word *authority* in the New Testament in *Strong's Exhaustive Concordance of the Bible* (the Greek dictionary)— index 1849—is *exousia*, which means "the right to control or govern dominion." Through Jesus, we have been given the right to control and take dominion over the power of the Holy Ghost. Jesus Christ has given to us that authority. He deputized and delegated to us his body of Christ, his people of prayer.

I can remember a time when I had to minister in Baltimore, Maryland. When I was there, God spoke to me about a young man I would see there. He showed me where the young man would be sitting and what this young man was going through. When I went to the church, just like God had showed me, the young man was there. As we ministered to the young man, he received his deliverance under the power of the Holy Ghost. The Spirit of God began to move in that place, and more people received their deliverance. As I was on my way home between Baltimore, Maryland, and Jersey City, New Jersey, I could feel a shift in the atmosphere. It felt like something was taking place in my body, and sure enough, there was.

A couple of days after I got home, my face was full of rashes, and I am a black woman with a dark-brown complexion. My skin had turned so bad to the point that I actually looked like a monster, and on top of that, I had a bite mark on my face near my cheek. I started using skin creams and eczema ointments, then it came to me that the devil had gotten mad with me because the gentleman and the others I ministered to received their deliverance. I got on the Word of God. I stood on Isaiah 53:5, "But He was wounded for our transgressions, He was bruised for our iniquities: the chastisement of our peace was upon Him; and by His stripes we are healed." I would confess every day by Jesus's stripes that I am healed. My skin was made whole. It was clear in the name of Jesus.

I did that about a month and would not stop. I stood on the Word of God for my healing, and before I knew it, my face had cleared up. The scripture tells us in James 4:7 KJV, "Submit yourselves therefore to God. Resist the Devil, and he will flee from you." I had to resist fear and worry and doubt and going back and forth to the doctor's office. There is nothing wrong with going to the dermatologist's office, but the medication was not helping me. I had to take a double dose of the

Word of God. His Word had to be my medication. The scripture also lets us know in 1 Peter 5:8–9 KJV, " 8 Be sober, be vigilant; because your adversary the Devil as a roaring lion, walks about seeking whom he may devour 9 Whom resist steadfast in the Faith."

When you are going through physical challenges, you must be steadfast in what the Word says about sickness. Refuse to worry, and use the Word of God to keep your mind under control. Don't allow yourself to let the devil in. Be watchful because the devil will try to tell you that your faith is not working. But, people of prayer, our faith is always working. We must tell people the need to resist speaking "Every year, I get allergies" or "I don't know if I will make it or not" or "Things never work for me." Saying things like that is from the devil. The scriptures tells us in Ephesians 6:10 KJV, "Finally, my Brethren, be strong in the Lord, and in the power of His Might." People of prayer, God does not want us to be strong in our own selves, like our self-will or positive thinking, but he wants us to be strong in him, be strong in the power of his might, be strong in the Word of God, which will give you the authority and power you need. Jesus already won the battle for us. We keep what he has attained for us.

This is the time that God wants his people of prayer to walk in revelation knowledge. Ephesians 6:11–18 KJV states, " 11 Put on the whole Armor of God, that you may be able to stand against the wiles of the Devil. 12 For we wrestle not against flesh and blood, against principalities, against powers, against the rulers of the darkness of this world against spiritual wickedness in high places 13 Wherefore take unto you the whole armor of God, that ye may be able to withstand in the evil day, and having done all, to stand. 14 Stand therefore, having your loins girt about with truth, and having on the breastplate of righteousness; 15 And your feet shod with the preparation of the gospel of peace; 16 Above all, taking the shield of faith, wherewith ye shall be able to quench all the fiery darts of the wicked [17] And take the helmet of salvation, and the sword of the Spirit, which is the word of God [18] Praying always with all prayer and supplication in the Spirit, and watching thereunto with all perseverance and supplication."

A prayer of will cannot be defeated with the armor God has given us. This is what we needed. The truth of the Word of God is a fact from his Word, which is what we need to comprehend what the Word of God is saying to us. The belt will hold everything else in place because the Word will help you stand against false teaching and religious bondage, and faith in the Word of Truth will pull down the strongholds from the devil's lies. When it comes to righteousness, we cannot be righteous without Jesus because of what he did on the cross and because of his resurrection and power. He sent the Holy Ghost; he made us righteous when we put him on, and we must obey his Word. He will fulfill everything he has said in his Word.

Our feet are shod with the gospel of peace. The only thing that will give peace in a world full of trouble is the gospel. We must faithfully and continually preach the gospel and teach the Word of God. When we take the shield of the faith, we are covered by Jesus and by his blood. There is nothing the devil can do to us when we are covered with the blood of Jesus. The devil will not and cannot come under the blood, and he cannot contaminate the blood. There is power in the blood of Jesus. The helmet of salvation, when we receive salvation, means deliverance, healing, and being set free from the wrath to come. We receive forgiveness of sin. The helmet of salvation protects our mind against the enemy who would come to bring lies and tell us that we are not saved and other kinds of lies.

The sword of the Spirit is the Word of God. The sword is used against what is impertinent or offensive every time the enemy comes with something that goes against the Word of God. You take the Word of God and cut to pieces every lie and thrust it into the devil. Every attack is done with the Word of God.

In the book of Genesis 18:16–33 KJV, it talks about how Abraham interceded for himself, for all saints, and for his nephew Lot.

> [16] And the men rose up from thence, and looked toward Sodom: and Abraham went with them to bring them on the way.
>
> [17] And the LORD said, Shall I hide from Abraham that thing which I do;
>
> [18] Seeing that Abraham shall surely become a great and mighty nation, and all the nations of the earth shall be blessed in him?
>
> [19] For I know him, that he will command his children and his household after him, and they shall keep the way of the LORD, to do justice and judgment; that the LORD may bring upon Abraham that which he hath spoken of him.
>
> [20] And the LORD said, because the cry of Sodom and Gomorrah is great, and because their sin is very grievous;
>
> [21] I will go down now, and see whether they have done altogether according to the cry of it, which is come unto me; and if not, I will know.
>
> [22] And the men turned their faces from thence, and went toward Sodom: but Abraham stood yet before the LORD.
>
> [23] And Abraham drew near, and said, Wilt thou also destroy the righteous with the wicked?
>
> [24] Peradventure there be fifty righteous within the city: wilt thou also destroy and not spare the place for the fifty righteous that are therein?

²⁵ That be far from thee to do after this manner, to slay the righteous with the wicked: and that the righteous should be as the wicked that be far from thee: Shall not the Judge of all the earth do right?

²⁶ And the LORD said, If I find in Sodom fifty righteous within the city, then I will spare all the place for their sakes.

²⁷ And Abraham answered and said, Behold now, I have taken upon me to speak unto the LORD, which am but dust and ashes:

²⁸ Peradventure there shall lack five of the fifty righteous: wilt thou destroy all the city for lack of five? And he said, If I find there forty and five, I will not destroy it.

²⁹ And he spake unto him yet again, and said, Peradventure there shall be forty found there. And he said, I will not do it for forty's sake.

³⁰ And he said unto him, Oh let not the LORD be angry, and I will speak: Peradventure there shall thirty be found there. And he said, I will not do it, if I find thirty there.

³¹ And he said, Behold now, I have taken upon me to speak unto the LORD: Peradventure there shall be twenty found there. And he said, I will not destroy it for twenty's sake.

³² And he said, Oh let not the LORD be angry, and I will speak yet but this once: Peradventure ten shall be found there. And he said, I will not destroy it for ten's sake.

³³ And the LORD went his way, as soon as he had left communing with Abraham: and Abraham returned unto his place.

Notice in the passage of scriptures what is said in verses 20, 21, and 22, "And the Lord said, Because the cry of Sodom and Gomorrah is great, and because their sin is very grievous." The sin of these two cites were so great that it became offensive and sickening to God. This means that there are some sins that cause corruption and contamination. This is why God took his angels with him. But notice this. Even though God was ready to invoke judgment because of transgressions, Abraham began to speak faith over his nephew and began to intercede for him. This is what brought God on the scene with Abraham. Intercession of faith caused things to turn around for Abraham's nephew.

The scriptures state in 2 Peter 2:7 KJV, "And delivered just Lot, vexed with the filthy conversation of the wicked." The prayer of intercession mixed with faith brought Lot out of a troubling and disturbing situation. Lot was being harassed by demons, being subjected to conversations, and being subjected to lewd, lustful acts of disrespect performed in front of him. This had vexed his spirit. This is why intercession was needed for him. The same is true for now. There may be family members, friends, coworkers, or enemies being vexed by demons because of some wrong decisions they have made. Intercession is needed to hold back judgment—to hold back cancer, AIDS, high blood pressure, low blood pressure, heart disease, kidney failure, stroke, lung disease, heart attacks, stomach problems, diabetes, headaches, problems with the eyes, or problems with their liver. Some may even have problems staying awake at night, and some cannot sleep because they suffer from insomnia, heart palpitations, tremors, problems with their glands and thyroids, etc. Whatever the devil wants to put on them, they need someone who will stand in the gap in prayer and faith and hold back judgment.

There are people who need people of prayer who will decree and declare the blessing on them so they will repent and have a change of heart. And they need to ask Jesus to come into their life so they will be saved, delivered, and set free. Father God, in the name of Jesus, I decree and declare that by your stripes, the healing power of God goes our way right now and brings healing on my family members, neighbors, and enemies. By your stripes, I decree and declare healing all over that body. Isaiah 53:5 KJV states, "But he was wounded for our transgressions, he was bruised for our iniquities: the chastisement of our peace was upon him; and with his stripes we are healed." This scripture lets us know that Jesus was wounded for our transgressions, meaning the whole world. Jesus Christ paid the price to redeem humanity from all manners of sicknesses and diseases on the cross.

It also means that he suffered so we would not have to suffer. He did not suffer for himself but for all. He suffered for all our iniquities, sins, and immoralities. He paid the price. Our sins placed Jesus on that cross, and because of what he did on the cross, we can decree and confess that "with his stripes, we are healed." If there is a family member who is battling with sickness, start interceding for them, and stand on the scriptures. Isaiah 53:5 KJV states, "He was wounded for our transgressions, he was bruised for our iniquities: the chastisement of our peace was upon him; and with his stripes we are healed." The scriptures lets us know in the book of Proverbs 18:21 KJV, "Death and life are in the power of the tongue: and they who love it shall eat the fruit thereof."

People of prayer must know they cannot constantly talk about doubt and unbelief and be an intercessor. An intercessor who talks about doubt and unbelief will bring forth death and be ineffective. But if you want to be effective, you must speak death to Satan and his demons and life to what the Word says. Father God, in the name of Jesus, I speak life to every cell in their body. In the name of Jesus, you stated in Exodus 15:26 KJV, "And said, If thou wilt diligently hearken to the voice of the LORD thy God, and wilt do that which is right in his sight, and wilt give ear to his commandments, and keep all his statutes, I will put none of these diseases upon thee, which I have brought upon the Egyptians: for I am the LORD that health thee."

The Word lets us know that if we diligently listen to the Word of God in our spirit and in our mind and confess and believe it by faith and speak it, he is the God who heals. The Word lets us know without a doubt that he is the Lord who heals every disease. None of those diseases will come to you and those you are interceding for. God is a miracle worker! Hallelujah! Hallelujah! With all that was going on in Sodom and Gomorrah, Lot came out, and there was no sickness in his body or his daughters' body.

The scriptures state in Matthew 8:16–17 KJV, "When the even was come, they brought unto him many that were possessed with devils: and he cast out the spirits with his word, and healed all that were sick: That it might be fulfilled which was spoken by Esaias the prophet, saying, Himself took our infirmities, and bare our sicknesses." Demons will cause people to be sick. Thank God, Abraham had faith in him to "call those things which be not as though as though they were" (Romans 4:17 KJV). Abraham had enough faith to call his nephew out of a dark situation and condition. Because Abraham worked his faith, it brought deliverance to his family. Jesus himself took our weaknesses. He took them for us. The faith in the Word brought about victory and blessing and not the curse.

The story in the book of Genesis 13:12 KJV reads, "Abram, dwelled in the land of Canaan, and Lot dwelled in the cities of the plain, and pitched his tent toward Sodom." Lot's selfness and self-will got him into trouble, just like how selfness today gets all humans in trouble. This stems from Adam's disobedience in the Garden of Eden in Genesis 2:15–17 KJV: "And the Lord God took the man, and put him into the

Garden of Eden to dress it and to keep it." Meaning God gave Adam stewardship over the garden. His job was to guard and protect what God had given him. "And the Lord God commanded the man, saying, 'Of every tree of the Garden you may freely eat. But of the Tree of the Knowledge of Good and Evil, you shall not eat of it.'" God specifically warned Adam of the tree of knowledge because this tree represented the deceitfulness of the world. It represents an attitude that is all about self and has nothing to do with God. Worldly wisdom that comes from man-made knowledge pertains to a system, a scheme of religious beliefs ordained by a man who is self-centered and filled with pride.

When Adam disobeyed God and ate of the tree of knowledge, Adam committed treachery, disloyalty, and betrayal, which is high treason. Genesis 3:9–10 KJV states, "And the LORD God called unto Adam, and said unto him, 'Where art thou?' And he said, 'I heard thy voice in the garden, and I was afraid, because I was naked; and I hid myself.'" Fear came in immediately, and Adam started looking out for himself. This is what Lot did. He started looking out for himself. Adam became self-centered and blamed the woman. Adam tried to cover himself. This is what sin does. It tells people that they can cover themselves and look out for number 1. Everything becomes about me, myself, and I. Even though Adam committed high treason and he incited and provoked God's judgment against him and his wife, the Lord interceded for him. The scriptures let us know in Genesis 3:21 KJV, "Unto Adam also and to his wife did the LORD God make coats of skins, and clothed them." Because of disobedience, Adam deserved judgment and the wrath of God. God could have killed Adam because God gave Adam dominion over the works of his hand. God covered Adam with his love. When God covered him with the animal skin, it covered and shielded him from what could have happened.

One of the most important things that prayer warriors need is to learn how to pray according to the Word of God. Prayer is a way of communicating with God, and it must be done according to the principles of faith in the Word of God. In the scripture in Hebrews 11:1 KJV, it says, "Now faith is the substance of things hoped for, the evidence of things not seen." The Word of God is your legal deed or document consisting of evidence of a right, especially of property. God has given us the right to stand on the Word that he spoke out of his mouth, and the Word is now in sixty-six books of the Bible. The Word of God is the title deed of the things you have been hoping for. It is God's promise. In other words, the Word of God is what we must have confidence in, and it gives us the legal right to stand on the promises of God. Faith has nothing to do with the five senses.

The Greek word for *faith* is, according to *Strong's Exhaustive Concordance*, *hypostasis* (*hyo* meaning "under" and *histeni* meaning "to stand"). It means that faith is the hypostasis, and it is what we stand under, the foundation that gives support. Faith in the Word means having confidence and trust in the scriptures. It is what you stand under and what you believe when you don't see anything happening in the natural world. You know that there is something happening in the spirit realm because you believe God's Word. Your confidence is in what he has said.

This is when things will begin to change here on earth and a shift will begin to take place. Prayer is not one of those "maybe God will hear me one day." No! Or a hit-and-miss! Believers should be getting answers to their prayers. People are in need of it now more than ever before. We must believe in God's capacity and his ability to do for us and the people we are praying for what we cannot do for ourselves and what they cannot do for themselves.

We are living in a time that is so superficial, insincere, and full of wickedness and immorality. One of the worst things was the belittling of our former president Barak Obama over whether he was born in the United States and whether he was a citizen in this country or not. This resulted in the former president releasing his birth certificate. Look at what's happened in the political arena. It was a pure joke with sadness. One was trying to degrade the other with disrespect, racism, and sexism. And they had no regard for women. According to Claire Cohen on June 30, 2017, at 6:09 a.m., "Fat. Pig. Dog. Slob. Disgusting animal. These are just some of the names that Donald Trump has called women" (p. 1). He also felt that no one would want to vote for Carly Fiorina because of her looks. He seemed to often be critical of them because of their looks or because he was being a sexist. In the race for president, it seemed like nothing tangible or substantial was being offered to people of other races and ethnic groups and to our children's education. It seemed as if he had brought in much racism.

The enemy has set out to kill black men just for sport. According to the *Guardian* (2015), "In the United States of America, more young black men are killed by police between the ages of 15–34 years old and despite making up only 2% of the total US population" (Lartey et al. 2015). The authors further stated that the police have gotten away with these crimes. Numerous black men have been killed, resulting in the movement of Black Lives Matters in 2013 after George Zimmerman killed an unarmed seventeen-year-old black youth in Florida. This unarmed youth was Trayvon Martin (Lee 2012). Other black males who were killed by police during 2016 were Eric Garner, Michael Brown, and Freddie Gray in Baltimore, Maryland (Huffington Post 2015).

Not only black males lost their lives to police brutality but also black women. Young black women are losing their lives, but it is less likely to make to the news. In 2015, fifteen black females lost their lives during police encounters (Abbey-Lambertz 2015). In one incident, Tanisha Anderson, thirty-seven years old, who resided in East Cleveland, lost her life when her mother called the police to investigate a mental health issue (bipolar disorder). The police came and restrained her, and she died shortly thereafter in police custody. She was slammed onto the pavement by the police, resulting in her respiratory organs being damaged. She died from injuries received when in custody of the police. So many blacks' lives have been lost due to systemic racism. The hearts of these males' and females' mothers have been broken. These mothers' hearts are in need of healing.

In the recent political race, there were no concerns for the poor, uneducated, unemployed, or the working-class citizens. Now a famous campaign slogan like "Building a wall and sending people back to their countries" is ridiculous. Many immigrants, their parents, and their grandparents worked very hard in this country to make a living. The United States has hit an all-time high crisis in suicide: "Suicide in the United States has surged to the highest levels in nearly 30 years, a federal data analysis has found, with increases in every age group except older adults" (Tavernise). And according to this article, suicide is abrupt when it comes to women. This research claims "there was a large increase among girls 10 to 14, whose suicide rate while still very low, had tripled" (Tavernise). Another disturbing finding is that "life expectancy declined slightly for white Americans in 2014, according to new federal data, a troubling sign that distress among younger and middle-age whites who are dying at ever-higher rates from drug overdoses is lowering average life spans for the white population as a whole" (Tavernise). The purpose of this book is to reveal that if there has ever been a time God needed intercessory prayer warriors who will pray the Word, then that time is now.

Listen, intercessors, we are living in a time of enlightenment. It's not about who is in office! Yes, President Donald Trump is in office, and we may not agree with his political party's philosophy on "Making America great again!" But listen, if God is not your source during this time, you can march all you want, call Trump names, talk about his family, wish he was not in office, or allow fear, anxiety, dread, worry, frustration, and anger to befall you. All these things will not change anything if God is not your source.

It has been noted in some papers that there could be some psychological health programs, some community and fine arts and global instruction and many other programs, including programs for children who are gifted and talented, and antibullying programs that will be cut. These are some of the programs that will be removed. This is proposed by our president, Trump. According to the *Washington Post* by Valerie Strauss, "The President may want to cut public educational school programs and social programs according to answer sheet analysis." Here are some details that aren't in the story. "First is a list in the budget documents of proposed discretionary programs targeted for elimination, which the documents say will save $5.9 billion, and following that are the given justifications for each. They were targeted, the documents say, because they 'achieved their original purpose, duplicate other programs, are narrowly focused, or are unable to demonstrate effectiveness'" (1). Also according to the *Post*, "$10.6 billion in cuts the administration want to make in federal education initiatives, and how it wants to reinvest part of the saving into efforts to promote school of choice" (1).

God has a plan and a purpose for our lives and the lives of our loved ones and those who are around us and are in the community and society. When we don't speak his Word and pray according to his Word, we cannot be effective in our homes, communities, schools, colleges, society, political field, etc. We abort the plans of God for our lives and the lives of others, and this must stop. Satan knows that God has a blueprint and purpose for men and women; therefore, he will keep Christians in their emotions, apprehension, and anxiety or worry about how to make ends meet. With all these budget cuts with different educational programs, we, as the body of Christ, need to arise and pay our tithe and offering like never before. Sow seeds and give them to ministries that are doing the work of Christ. It is amazing how Satan will keep people of God in their feeling when it comes to giving the things of God. Yet people have no problem if they want to get their nails done or get that weave or go and play that Powerball or lottery ticket. This lets us know that God is interested in our economic resources, and through these resources, we can help get young people off the streets and get them saved and let them see a better future for themselves.

According to the scripture in Ezekiel 22:30 KJV, "And I sought for a man among them, that should make up the hedge, and stand in the gap before me for the land, that I should not destroy it: but I found none." This scripture reveals the heart of God toward his people. Israel is an elected nation to bring forth the glorious Messiah. God had done so much for Israel. He loved them and showed them mercy and grace. When they needed protection, he protected them. When they needed healing, he healed them and delivered them. When they needed food, he gave them manna. Whatever they needed, he provided for them. But during this time, Israel had entered into rebelliousness toward God. Not one person was praying and standing on the Word of God. This is such a sad indictment against the people of God.

God was looking for someone who would stand in the gap and arise, intervene, and intercede for the people in prayer. And this would give God permission and authorization to come into the situation and bring love, healing, and deliverance. This is what is happening now in the twenty-first century. God is looking for intercessors who will arise and use the Word of God in prayer and stand in the gap for others to see them delivered from the bondage of sin and the oppression of Satan. As an intercessor, we cannot be selfish, just praying for people we know and not those we do not know because of the perilous time.

Joshua 1:8 KJV states, "This book of law shall not depart out of my mouth but thou shall meditate therein day and night, that you may observe to do according to all that is written therein: for then thou shalt make thy prosperous, and then thou shalt have good success." What God is saying to Joshua is, in order to lead the people into success, this will only come from mediating on the Word of God. If we, as the body of Christ, as prayer warriors, as intercessors, want to lead people through prayer to the kingdom of God, we must seek God for his wisdom in prayer in how to deal with individuals wisely. How to discern and recognize what is going on in their life comes from spending time in the Word.

When we, as intercessors, spend time in the Word, we will be ready to fight against demons who are ready to destroy our faith in God and that person or persons we are praying for. As we mediate on the Word, it will begin to change our inner image. The devil wants people of prayer to just see defeat, but the devil is a liar. Shout out right now, "I see victory in Jesus's name!" The enemy does not want the people of God to use scriptures to counterattack the enemy. The more you use the Word, the more confident you will become.

The story of Joshua 1:2 KJV says, "Moses My servant is dead; now therefore arise, go over this Jordan you, and all this people, unto the land which I do give them, even the children of Israel." When God told this to Joshua, he could have gotten in fear right then. As people of prayer, we must guard our minds against the spirts of fear that want to try to intimidate us and depress and oppress us and to make us doubt God's Word. That is the plan of the enemy. He does not want intercessors to have faith in his Word. The scriptures says in 2 Corinthians 10:5 KJV, "Casting down imaginations, and every high thing that exalted itself against the knowledge of God, and bringing into captivity every thought to the obedience of Christ."

More than likely, the thoughts that are coming to you are evil thoughts, just like they were coming to Joshua. Thoughts dictate our actions, our images, and our feelings, and what we are observing in our mind. The moment it was revealed to Joshua that Moses was dead, right then and there, he had to take authority over his mind and he began to cast down imaginations—imagination that says "This is too hard! Lord, why did you call me to do this? Why did you tell me? Why did you show me?" Your thoughts will control your actions. The devil paints a picture in your mind that what God said can't be done or that you are the wrong person or that this must not be God! There are people in this world, even in the twenty-first century, who believe that God, our Lord Jesus Christ, is in charge of everything that happens in the world. And they blame him if things don't go right and think that God can't do anything. That is not true. I repeat. This type of thinking is not true.

There are people who are agnostic, and some who are atheists. According to Dicionary.com (2017), *agnostic* is "a person who holds that the existence of the ultimate cause, as God, and the essential nature of things are unknown and unknowable, that human knowledge is limited to experience." And according to Dictionary.com, an *atheist* is "a person who denies or disbelieves the existence of a supreme being or beings." Dicionary.com says that *deism* is "the disbelief in the existence of a supreme being, specifically of a creator who does not intervene in the universe." The term is used chiefly of an intellectual movement of the seventeenth and eighteenth centuries that accepted the existence of a creator on the basis of reason but rejected belief in a supernatural deity who interacts with humankind. All these types of philosophies and philosophical worldviews that are just mentioned above are man-made thoughts that go against the Word of God.

The scriptures says that as prayer warriors in 2 Corinthians 10:3–5, "For though we walk in the flesh, we do not war after the flesh: For the weapons of our warfare are not carnal, but mighty through God to the pulling down of strong holds; Casting down imaginations, and every high thing that exalteth itself against the knowledge of God, and bringing into captivity every thought to the obedience of Christ." Verse 3 lets us know that we, as humans, live in this flesh, not glorified bodies. Verse 4 means we do not do war in our own natural ability, for example, cursing, fist fighting, or putting individuals down on Facebook, Twitter, etc. But the Holy Ghost, through the power of prayer, helps to aid and assist us in this spiritual war that we are in. This scripture lets us know that it takes the scriptures and faith in the Word of God, as we appropriate the scriptures as the weapon we use against what we are fighting in the world, the spiritual host of wickedness, this world system, which is the devil. We must know the Word of God in order to know the will of God. Verse 5 lets the believer know that we, as the believers, must cast down philosophies that turn into human strongholds and worldviews that go against what Jesus did on the cross. Also, these are highly exalted thoughts of man-made opinions that go against the scriptures. God created man in his image, but after the Fall, man lost sight of who God created him to be.

The Bible lets us know in Genesis 1 that in order to be a person of prayer, you must be willing to give the Lord Jesus Christ the consent, the approval, and the agreement or permission to work through you through prayer. God is looking for prayer warriors to come into agreement with him with what the Word says about a situation. This is why it says in the scripture in Ezekiel 22:30 KJV, "And I sought for a man among them that should make up the hedge, and stand in the gap before me for the land, that I should not destroy it: but I found none." God is saying he is looking for someone who will come into agreement with what his Word says and become one with him through Jesus Christ. So many times, we have our own opinion about things and leave Jesus out of it. We can no longer be that way. When we are born-again, and when we are filled with the Holy Ghost, we already have access to everything we need to be his children in heaven. But the problem is unbelief and not giving him the permission, including weaves, nails, and competition with one another. Satan wants individuals to be locked into themselves, to be selfish. There is a spiritual force that is coming against us more and more. This is spiritual warfare, and it will take women of God, intercessory prayer warriors, to rise up and take their rightful authority in this place here on earth. There is a spiritual opposition that we must wage war against.

The Bible tells us this in John 10:10 KJV, "The thief cometh not, but for to steal, and to kill, and to destroy: I am come that they might have life, and that they might have it more abundantly." Who is the thief? It is Satan. The Greek word for *thief* in *Strong's Exhaustive Concordance* (2812) is *kléptēs*, which means "a thief who steals by stealth (in secret) rather than in the open with violence" (WS, 591). He places small seeds that becomes ungodly thoughts in your mind, which go against the Word of God. He then takes these thoughts and starts to pull you in, and if you are not careful, you will begin to fantasize over these thoughts because he wants you to think that there is nothing wrong with thinking this way. And know if there are no resisting feelings, they become bigger and bigger. Now this is where Satan starts to rip people off and destroy their lives.

Individuals believe that certain things in this society will bring them fulfillment and peace. The devil uses suicide, drugs, alcohol, pornography, adultery, fornication, abuse of oneself, abuse of women, abuse of children, poverty, low self-esteem, fear, anger, doubt, unbelief, sickness, cancer, high blood pressure, low blood pressure, kidney failure, diabetes, skin disorders, and blood disorders for the murder and destruction of our children. It's time to wake up, speak up, and stand up in our rightful authority.

The second part of that same scripture says, "I am come that they may have life and have it more abundantly" (John 10:10 KJV). The great I Am is the god of grace. Satan uses and markets false gods to give individuals hopes and dreams that are false. But the problem remains that there are some people who don't know that he is a master of deception, who wears a mask to fool individuals. Thank God, Jesus Christ came to redeem the fallen humankind and give them life, which the enemy came to steal from man. Father, in the name of Jesus, you are the great I Am! Father, you are everything that we need you to be. And, Father God, we thank you that you are our protector, in Jesus's name. This is why every day as prayer warriors, we must start our day off with the Word of God.

Please repeat this prayer after me. Father God, in Jesus's name, as we start our day off, we want to give you the glory that only you deserve. In Jesus's name, we arise this morning to take our rightful authority. Today, in Jesus's name, Father, we stand on and confess Joshua 1:8 KJV, "Father God, I decree and declare this book of the law, which is the word of God, shall not depart out of my mouth: but you shall meditate therein day and night, that you may observe to do add according to all that is written therein: for then you shall make your way prosperous and then you shall have good success." There is another translation that says that "thou will be able to deal wisely in the affairs of life." It is of uttermost importance that we build our life on the principles of the Word of God. The principles of the Word is the only thing we can live by and that give us the wisdom. We need to cope with the affairs of life. It will take wisdom from God. Women, one of the most important things we need to realize in prayer is that it is the only way.

In the beginning in the book of Genesis 1:26 KJV, it states, "And God said, 'Let us make man in Our image, and after our likeness." It means making mankind a speaking spirit. They will be able to have fellowship and relationship with God. "And let them have dominion over the fish of the sea, and over the fowls of the air, and over the cattle, and over the Earth, and over every creeping thing that creeps upon the Earth."

CPSIA information can be obtained
at www.ICGtesting.com
Printed in the USA
LVHW02*1551260718
585038LV00007B/65/P

Travel phrasebooks collection
«Everything Will Be Okay!»

T&P Books Publishing

PHRASEBOOK

— SERBIAN —

By Andrey Taranov

THE MOST IMPORTANT PHRASES

This phrasebook contains
the most important
phrases and questions
for basic communication
Everything you need
to survive overseas

T&P BOOKS

Phrasebook + 3000-word dictionary

English-Serbian phrasebook & topical vocabulary

By Andrey Taranov

The collection of "Everything Will Be Okay" travel phrasebooks published by T&P Books is designed for people traveling abroad for tourism and business. The phrasebooks contain what matters most - the essentials for basic communication. This is an indispensable set of phrases to "survive" while abroad.

This book also includes a small topical vocabulary that contains roughly 3,000 of the most frequently used words. Another section of the phrasebook provides a gastronomical dictionary that may help you order food at a restaurant or buy groceries at the store.

T&P Books Publishing
www.tpbooks.com

ISBN: 978-1-78492-425-6

This book is also available in E-book formats.
Please visit www.tpbooks.com or the major online bookstores.

FOREWORD

The collection of "Everything Will Be Okay" travel phrasebooks published by T&P Books is designed for people traveling abroad for tourism and business. The phrasebooks contain what matters most - the essentials for basic communication. This is an indispensable set of phrases to "survive" while abroad.

This phrasebook will help you in most cases where you need to ask something, get directions, find out how much something costs, etc. It can also resolve difficult communication situations where gestures just won't help.

This book contains a lot of phrases that have been grouped according to the most relevant topics. The edition also includes a small vocabulary that contains roughly 3,000 of the most frequently used words. Another section of the phrasebook provides a gastronomical dictionary that may help you order food at a restaurant or buy groceries at the store.

Take "Everything Will Be Okay" phrasebook with you on the road and you'll have an irreplaceable traveling companion who will help you find your way out of any situation and teach you to not fear speaking with foreigners.

TABLE OF CONTENTS

T&P Books Publishing